Slow Cooker 101

MASTER THE SLOW COOKER WITH 101 GREAT RECIPES

EDITED BY **Perrin Davis**

CONTENTS

PASTA AND RICE ENTRÉES 94

SIDE DISHES.. 102

INTRODUCTION

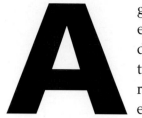gate Surrey Books wants to help everyone, but especially kitchen beginners, learn how to explore different kinds of food and cooking. We are proud to introduce the *101* series, which aims to provide rewarding, successful, and fun cooking experiences for everyone, from novices to more experienced cooks. *Slow Cooker 101: Master the Slow Cooker with 101 Great Recipes* is one of the first books in this series, and it offers readers not only delicious recipes but also useful information about shopping for equipment, ingredients, kitchen essentials, and seasonings. Getting started with your slow cooker can be intimidating, but we'll demystify the process for you. So whether you're using your slow cooker because you simply don't have time after work to put a dinner together, or you're interested in the slow cooker because of the wonderful flavors that can develop when the heat is low and slow, *Slow Cooker 101* is a great place to start.

Most of the recipes in these *101* series books come from a wide range of Agate Surrey authors and editors. Contributors to *Slow Cooker 101* include Sue Spitler, editor of the "1,001" series that includes titles like *1,001 Low-Fat Vegetarian Recipes* and *1,001 Best Slow-Cooker Recipes*, and Anupy Singla, author of *The Indian Slow Cooker*.

Slow Cooker 101 recipes were selected to provide a starting point for anyone beginning their slow-cooking journey. The collection includes a variety of cuisines (Italian, Mexican, Spanish, Asian, and Indian, to name a few). Most of the recipes are simple, although a handful of them are more advanced; you'll find that all are easy to follow.

A TASTE OF WHAT YOU'LL FIND IN THIS BOOK

This book contains lots of fantastic main-dish options in the Beef, Pork, Chicken, Lamb, and Seafood Entrees chapters. Don't miss great dinner-party options like Lamb Biryani, Beef and Mushroom Stroganoff, and Poached Salmon with Lemon-Caper Sauce, as well as delicious family pleasers like Pulled Chicken Sandwiches and Picadillo Tacos. Hearty Philly Cheesesteak and Italian Beef sandwiches will

put smiles on everyone's face, and Greek Pitas are a big favorite in our house.

In the Side Dishes chapter, check out delicious dishes like Brazilian Black Bean Bake, Ginger-Garlic Eggplant, Potatoes Gratin, and Goat Cheese Polenta. You'll love letting the slow cooker do all the work on holidays when you use it to make our Candied Yams or Real Mashed Potatoes—and free up the stove and oven to make your other favorites!

Winter Vegetable Risotto, Paella, and Seven-Layer Lasagna are just a few of the tasty offerings in the Pasta and Rice chapter. Need to feed an army of kids? Look no further than our Ultimate Mac 'n' Cheese on page 96.

But before you get started cooking some of these great recipes, make sure you're up to speed on some slow cooking basics, and that your kitchen and pantry are ready to go!

SLOW COOKING BASICS

Slow cookers have been around since the middle of the last century, but Rival's Crock Pot brand really took off in 1971. The name has become interchangeable with the slow cooker, but today countless other manufacturers make slow cookers. They all work pretty much the same—there's a round or oval stoneware, porcelain, or ceramic pot with a lid, usually made of glass or clear plastic (to prevent curiosity from getting the better of you), all set in a metal heating element that cooks food at a low temperature. Slow cooker dishes always contain at least a little liquid, and once the dish begins cooking, the liquid begins to turn into water vapor, which helps create a firm seal for the lid. The vapor condenses into liquid that returns to the food, increasing as time goes by. That is why only a little liquid is added at start of cooking.

Slow cookers differ greatly in size. The most common size is 3½ or 4-quart, and some recipes in this book call for a 6-quart cooker. You can buy a slow cooker today with capacities as low as 16 ounces and as large as more than 7 quarts. Most cookers have two heat settings—high (about 280°F) and low (170°F)—and you'll find those designations in each recipe in this book.

The cooking process in a slow cooker is really quite simple. You place your ingredients (which, as mentioned above, must always include some liquid) in the pot and turn the device on, setting it to either high or low. The heating element reaches the desired temperature and stays there for as many hours as you have specified on the device's timer. After that time is achieved, most slow cookers will shut off and go to a "keep warm" setting, which keeps the food at about 165°F until you are ready to serve.

One of the greatest advantages of the slow cooker is its ability to turn tough, inexpensive cuts of meat with lots of connective tissue into delicious, succulent morsels. You'll see that many of this book's recipes call for relatively inexpensive meat cuts. Cooking at such a low temperature means that your food won't burn—so you won't waste it! Slow cookers are also very energy efficient and keep your kitchen cool on a hot summer day.

KITCHEN EQUIPMENT BASICS

If you are a new cook, or it's been a while since you've spent time in the kitchen, here is some helpful information that will make it easy to jump into *Slow Cooker 101* recipes. The following is not necessarily slow-cooking specific, but if you have the following equipment, you will be prepared to make almost any recipe in this book.

Appliances

We're sure you know this already, but your kitchen should include the following standard set of appliances.

Pretty Much Mandatory

- Slow cooker (4 to 6 quart)

- Refrigerator/freezers (set to about 34°F to 38°F, or as cold as you can get it without freezing vegetables or drinks)

- Freezer (if yours is not frost-free, you'll periodically need to unplug it to defrost your snow-filled box)

- Stove/oven (make sure the oven stays very clean, as burnt foods and other odors can affect the taste of your food), because you'll need it for browning some meats before starting a slow-cooked dish

- Microwave (again, make sure it's clean and ready for use), because it's great for defrosting

- Blender (and not just for beverages and soups—you can use it in place of a food processor or an immersion blender in many instances)

- Hand mixer (well, you can always stir by hand, but sometimes, the hand mixer is indispensable)

Optional

- Food processor
- Immersion blender
- Stand mixer

Pots and Pans

The following are useful basic equipment for any kitchen.

- Stockpot (8 to 10 quarts)
- Dutch oven (5 to 6 quarts)
- Glass casserole dish (2 quart)
- Pancake griddle
- Large stockpot with lid (6 to 8 quarts)
- Large skillet with lid (10 to 12 inches in diameter)
- Medium skillet with lid (7 to 8 inches in diameter)
- Medium saucepan with lid (2 or 3 quarts)
- Small saucepan with lid (1 quart)
- Square cake pan (8 or 9 inches)
- Rectangular cake pan (13 × 9 inches)
- 2 loaf pans (8 inches)
- Muffin pan (12 muffins)
- Pie pan (9 inches in diameter)
- 2 baking sheets

General Utensils

These are recommended basics for any kitchen.

- Knives: Chef's knife, serrated knife, and paring knife

- Measuring cups for both dry and liquid measures

- Measuring spoons

- Mixing bowls (two or three, ranging from 1 or 2 quarts to 5 or 6 quarts)

- Wooden spoons, slotted spoon, rubber or silicone spatula, ladle, whisk, tongs, and a large metal "flipper" for hamburgers and similar foods

- Colander

- Cheese grater

- Citrus zester

- Salt and pepper mills

- Kitchen scissors

- Vegetable peeler

- Can opener

- Cooling rack

- Kitchen timer

- Cutting boards—at least two, so you have one for vegetables and cooked foods and one for raw meats

- Pot holders

- Kitchen towels

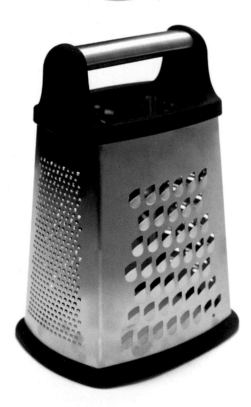

Storage and Cleaning

Either in a handy drawer or on a shelf, make sure you have all of these items within easy reach.

- Plastic or glass storage containers (5 to 10, varying sizes)
- Aluminum foil
- Plastic wrap
- Parchment paper
- Small baggies
- Large baggies
- Muffin pan liners

BASIC INGREDIENTS LIST FOR SLOW COOKING

This section includes the basics that you should have on hand, but this is by no means a comprehensive list for every recipe in this book. If you have these ingredients as a starting point, however, you'll be in great shape to tackle almost any of the *Slow Cooker 101* recipes!

Seasonings and Flavorings

- Basil
- Bay leaves
- Beef, chicken, and vegetable bouillon cubes or vegetable base (just add water to either to make instant vegetable stock)
- Cayenne pepper
- Chili powder
- Cumin
- Dry mustard

- Garlic powder
- Ground cinnamon
- Ground ginger
- Ground nutmeg
- Hot red pepper flakes
- Italian seasoning
- Oregano
- Paprika
- Kosher salt
- Vanilla extract
- White pepper
- Freshly ground black pepper

Condiments

- Apple cider vinegar
- Balsamic vinegar
- Honey
- Hot pepper sauce
- Ketchup
- Mustard
- Olive oil
- Red wine vinegar
- Rice vinegar
- Soy sauce
- Vegetable oil
- White wine vinegar
- Worcestershire sauce

Baking

- Cornstarch
- Baking powder
- Baking soda
- Margarine or butter
- Vegetable shortening
- Maple syrup
- Molasses
- Whole or 2% milk
- Granulated sugar
- Light and dark brown sugar
- Unbleached all-purpose flour
- Unbleached whole wheat flour
- Unbleached white spelt flour

General

- White rice
- Brown rice
- Garlic

- Pasta
- Onions
- Potatoes
- Peanut butter
- Canned tomatoes
- Raisins
- Tomato sauce
- Beef, chicken, and vegetable broth

COMMON COOKING TERMS

You probably are quite familiar with most of these terms, and most won't be necessary for slow cooking ... because after all, that's why you're using the slow cooker! But we know that you've got other stuff to make, and the slow cooker can't contain every dish on your menu. If this is your first time cooking or it's been a while since you've been in the kitchen, here is a quick refresher:

- **Brown:** To cook a meat at a high temperature for a very brief period of time in order to seal in the juices and add a tremendous amount of flavor. You'll see this in a lot of this book's slow-cooking recipes, because it's a tremendous flavor booster. Browning should take no more than two or three minutes on each side and is done before thoroughly cooking the meat —say, for example, in a slow cooker! It may be tempting to skip this step when putting your ingredients in the slow cooker, but please don't ... it's really worth the few minutes in terms of the flavor and texture of the meat once your recipe is complete.

- **Bake:** To cook food with dry heat, usually in the oven at a specified temperature.

- **Boil:** To cook food in boiling water (212°F) on the stovetop.

- **Blanch:** A technique that involves immersing food in boiling water for a brief period of time and then immediately transferring into an ice bath in order to stop the cooking process. Blanching is an excellent technique for quickly cooking tender vegetables, as it helps them retain their firmness, crispness, and color.

- **Braise:** This technique is a combination of browning the surface of meat, which means to cook at a high temperature for a short amount of time, followed by cooking at a lower temperature in a covered pot with liquid for a longer period of time— like in the slow cooker!

- **Broil:** To cook over a high heat at a specified distance from the heat source, usually in the oven or in the "broiler" part of the oven.

- **Deep fry:** To cook food by immersing it in preheated oil.

- **Grill:** To cook over an open flame on a metal framework, gridiron, or other cooking surface.

- **Roast:** To cook in an oven in an uncovered dish, usually resulting in a well-browned surface that seals in juices and flavors.

- **Sauté:** To cook food over a medium-high or high heat in a skillet or sauté pan in a small amount of oil, water, stock, or other liquid.

- **Steam:** To cook food with steam, usually in a steamer rack or basket positioned over (but not immersed in) a pan containing a small amount of water.

- **Stir-fry:** To cook over high heat with a small amount of oil; usually requires regular stirring as food is cooking. It can be used for several kinds of dishes and is often associated with Asian fare.

GENERAL COOKING TIPS

No matter what you're cooking or how many people you're serving, a few universal rules of the kitchen will make your life easier. The following is a list of our recommendations for the novice cook. These great habits will ensure fewer mistakes, less stress, and ultimately more delicious food.

- **Read every recipe from beginning to end, at least twice, before you start cooking.** This will help to ensure that you understand how it should be made and what you need to make it.

- **Set up your ingredients, pots, pans, and utensils before you begin to prepare the recipes.** We never start a recipe until we have every ingredient on the counter in front of us. (If possible, we also premeasure all the ingredients and have them ready to add, because there's nothing worse than accidentally dumping half a box of kosher salt into an almost-finished recipe.) If you know you'll need a greased pan in step 4, grease it and set it aside before you even get started.

- **Keep a grocery list and a pen attached to the refrigerator.** If you go to the grocery store without a specific list of what you need, you're likely to forget at least a few items.

- **Clean up as you go.** If you take the time to clean your dishes as you're cooking, you'll find that you will have more space to work in and less to do after the meal is done.

- **Time the meal.** It can be complicated to cook multiple recipes at once and make sure that everything ends up finishing at roughly the same time. Make sure you allow for enough time for everything to get done, and for recipes to be cooked simultaneously.

- **Be careful.** It sounds silly, but never forget that you're working with high-temperature appliances and cookware and sharp utensils! Use proper precaution when lifting lids, turning pans, and straining vegetables.

- **Have fun!** We hope you enjoy learning how to cook these recipes and sharing them with others.

MAKING FOIL HANDLES

The use of foil handles facilitates removal of whole roasts and chicken from the slow cooker. Cut 2 long strips of heavy duty foil that will fit into the slow cooker, going across the bottom and extending to the top of the sides of the crock. Fold the strips in half 2 or 3 times to increase their strength; fit into slow cooker and add the roast or chicken.

BEEF STEWS & ENTRÉES

BEEF AND MUSHROOM STROGANOFF

Serve in shallow bowls with warm crusty bread to soak up the juices.

4 ENTRÉE SERVINGS

INGREDIENTS

1 pound (454 gm) lean beef round steak, cut into strips (½-inch [1-cm])
1½ cups (354 mL) beef broth
8 ounces (224 gm) mushrooms, sliced
½ cup (118 mL) chopped onion
¼ cup (59 gm) chopped shallots or green onions
1 clove garlic, minced
½–1 cup (118–236 mL) sour cream
2 tablespoons (30 mL) cornstarch
Salt and pepper, to taste

1. Combine all ingredients, except sour cream, cornstarch, salt, and pepper, in slow cooker; cover and cook on low 6 to 8 hours. Stir in combined sour cream and cornstarch, stirring 2 to 3 minutes. Season to taste with salt and pepper.

TERIYAKI BEEF AND BROCCOLI STEW

The stew can also be served over rice, pasta, or any grain.

4 ENTRÉE SERVINGS

INGREDIENTS

12–16 ounces (336–545 gm) lean beef round steak, cut into thin strips (½-inch [1-cm])
1 cup (236 mL) beef broth
1 medium onion, cut into thin wedges
2 carrots, sliced
1 tablespoon (15 mL) minced gingerroot
2 tablespoons (30 mL) teriyaki sauce
2 cups (473 mL) small broccoli florets
2 tablespoons (30 mL) cornstarch
¼ cup (59 mL) cold water
Salt and pepper, to taste
8 ounces noodles, cooked, warm

1. Combine all ingredients, except broccoli, cornstarch, water, salt, pepper, and noodles, to slow cooker; cover and cook on low 6 to 8 hours, adding broccoli during last 30 minutes. Turn heat to high and cook 10 minutes; stir in combined cornstarch and water, stirring 2 to 3 minutes. Season to taste with salt and pepper; serve over noodles.

GREEK BEEF AND LENTIL STEW

Lentils and fresh vegetables partner deliciously in this easy stew.

6 ENTRÉE SERVINGS

INGREDIENTS

1 pound (454 gm) boneless beef eye of round, cubed (¾-inch [2 cm])
3 cups (708 mL) beef broth
1 can (14½ ounces [406 gm]) diced tomatoes, undrained
2 cups (473 mL) each: cubed Idaho potatoes, cut green beans
1 cup (236 mL) each: dried lentils, chopped onion, green bell pepper
2 teaspoons (10 mL) minced garlic
1 teaspoon (5 mL) each: dried oregano and mint leaves
½ teaspoon 2.5 mL) each: ground turmeric, coriander
1 cup (236 mL) cubed zucchini
Salt and pepper, to taste

1. Combine all ingredients, except zucchini, salt, and pepper, in 6-quart slow cooker; cover and cook on low 6 to 8 hours, adding zucchini during last 30 minutes. Season to taste with salt and pepper.

BARBECUED BEEF AND BEAN STEW

This spicy barbecued beef and bean dinner is sure to please!

6 ENTRÉE SERVINGS

INGREDIENTS

1 pound (454 gm) lean beef round steak, cut into strips (½-inch [1-cm])

3 cans (15 ounces [424 gm] each) kidney beans, rinsed, drained

1 can (8 ounces [224 gm]) tomato sauce

½ cup (118 mL) mild or medium salsa

1½ cups (354 mL) finely chopped onions

2 cloves garlic, minced

2 tablespoons (30 mL) cider vinegar

2–3 (30–45 mL) tablespoons packed brown sugar

2–3 (10–15 mL) teaspoons (10–15 mL) chili powder

2 teaspoons (10 mL) Worcestershire sauce

1 cup (236 mL) whole kernel corn

Salt and pepper, to taste

1. Combine all ingredients, except corn, salt, and pepper, in slow cooker; cover and cook on low 6 to 8 hours, stirring in corn during last 30 minutes. Season to taste with salt and pepper.

ROSEMARY BEEF STEW

Fragrant rosemary is the highlight of this delicious stew.

6 ENTRÉE SERVINGS

INGREDIENTS

1½ pounds (678 gm) lean beef stew meat, cubed
1½ cups (354 mL) beef broth
1 can (8 ounces [224 gm]) tomato sauce
2 tablespoons (30 mL) dry sherry (optional)
3 cups (708 mL) cut green beans
1 cup (236 mL) finely chopped onion
½ cup (118 mL) each: sliced carrots, celery
1 large clove garlic, minced
1 teaspoon (5 mL) dried rosemary leaves
1 bay leaf
1–2 tablespoons (15–30 mL) cornstarch
¼ cup (59 mL) cold water
Salt and pepper, to taste
4 cups (.95 L) cooked rice, warm

1. Combine all ingredients, except cornstarch, water, salt, pepper, and rice, in slow cooker; cover and cook on low 6 to 8 hours. Turn heat to high and cook 10 minutes; stir in combined cornstarch and water, stirring 2 to 3 minutes. Discard bay leaf; season to taste with salt and pepper; serve over rice.

WINE-BRAISED BEEF STEW

Slow cooking gives this dish a rich flavor. A good-quality Chianti would be an excellent wine choice.

6 ENTRÉE SERVINGS

INGREDIENTS

1½ pounds (678 gm) boneless beef round steak, cubed
1 cup (236 mL) each: beef broth, tomato sauce
½ cup (118 mL) dry red wine or beef broth
2 cups (473 mL) sliced mushrooms
1 cup (236 mL) chopped onion
½ cup (118 mL) thinly sliced celery
12 baby carrots
6 small potatoes, halved
1 teaspoon (5 mL) each: minced garlic, dried thyme leaves
2 large bay leaves
1–2 tablespoons (15–30 mL) cornstarch
¼ cup (59 mL) cold water
Salt and pepper, to taste

1. Combine all ingredients, except cornstarch, water, salt, and pepper, in 6-quart slow cooker; cover and cook on low 6 to 8 hours. Turn heat to high and cook 10 minutes; stir in combined cornstarch and water, stirring 2 to 3 minutes. Discard bay leaves; season to taste with salt and pepper.

WHOLE-MEAL POT ROAST >

Pot roast with vegetables can't be beat for a cold weather meal—add the wine, or not, for extra flavor.

8 SERVINGS

INGREDIENTS

1 beef chuck roast (about 3 pounds [1.36 kg)
2 large onions, halved and sliced
1 package (1 ounce [28 gm]) onion soup mix
1 pound (454 gm) carrots, thickly sliced
6–8 medium red potatoes, unpeeled
½ small head cabbage, cut into 6–8 wedges
Salt and pepper
½ cup (118 mL) dry red wine or beef broth

1. Place beef on onions in 6-quart slow cooker and sprinkle with soup mix. Arrange vegetables around beef and sprinkle lightly with salt and pepper; add wine, cover and cook on low 6 to 8 hours. Serve beef and vegetables with broth, or make gravy.

Note: To make gravy, measure broth and pour into small saucepan; heat to boiling. For every cup of broth, whisk in 2 tablespoons (30 mL) flour mixed with ¼ cup (59 mL) cold water, whisking until thickened, about 1 minute.

BARBECUED BRISKET

This delicious brisket is prepared with an easy Spice Rub and slow cooked to perfection with barbecue sauce.

10 SERVINGS

INGREDIENTS

1 beef brisket, fat trimmed (about 3 pounds [1.36 kg])
Spice Rub (recipe follows)
2 cups (473 mL) barbecue sauce
¼ cup (59 mL) each: red wine vinegar, packed light brown
    sugar
2 medium onions, sliced
½ cup (118 mL) water
1 pound (454 gm) fettuccine, cooked, warm

1. Rub brisket with Spice Rub and place in slow cooker; pour in combined remaining ingredients, except fettuccine. Cover and cook on low 6 to 8 hours, turning heat to high during last 20 to 30 minutes. Remove brisket to serving platter and let stand, covered with foil, 10 minutes. Slice and serve with barbecue sauce and onions over fettuccine.

SPICE RUB

MAKES ABOUT 2 TABLESPOONS (30 ML)

INGREDIENTS

2 tablespoons (30 mL) minced parsley
1 teaspoon (5 mL) minced garlic
½ teaspoon (2.5 mL) each: seasoned salt, ground ginger,
    nutmeg, and pepper

1. Mix all ingredients.

VARIATIONS

Barbecued Beef Sandwiches—Make recipe as above, omitting fettuccine; shred brisket with 2 forks and mix with barbecue mixture; spoon beef onto bottoms of toasted hoagie rolls and top with coleslaw and bun tops.

Pulled Pork Sandwiches—Make recipe as above, substituting bone-less pork loin for the brisket and omitting fettuccine; shred pork with 2 forks and mix with barbecue mixture. Serve in toasted burger buns with dill pickles.

JUST PLAIN MEAT LOAF

Moist, the way meat loaf should be, with plenty of leftovers for sand-wiches, too! Serve with mashed potatoes.

6 SERVINGS

INGREDIENTS

1½ pounds (681 gm) lean ground beef
1 cup (236 mL) quick-cooking oats
½ cup (118 mL) 2% milk
1 egg
¼ cup (59 mL) ketchup or chili sauce
½ cup (118 mL) each: chopped onion, green bell pepper
1 teaspoon (5 mL) each: minced garlic, dried Italian sea-soning, salt
½ (2.5 mL) teaspoon pepper

1. Make foil handles (see p. 23) and fit into slow cooker. Mix all ingredients until blended; pat mixture into a loaf shape and place in slow cooker, making sure sides of loaf do not touch crock. Insert meat thermometer so tip is in center of loaf; cover and cook on low until meat thermometer registers 170°F (77°C), 6 to 7 hours. Remove, using foil handles, and let stand, loosely covered with foil, 10 minutes.

Note—Meat loaf can also be cooked in a 9 x 5-inch (22.5 x 12.5 cm) loaf pan or two smaller loaf pans, if they fit in your slow cooker; place pans on a rack.

VARIATIONS

Italian Meat Loaf—Make recipe as above, adding ¼ cup (1 ounce [28 gm]) grated Parmesan cheese, ½ cup (2 ounces [56 gm]) shred-ded mozzarella cheese, and 2 tablespoons (30 mL) chopped pitted black olives. At the end of cooking time, top with 2 tablespoons (30 mL) seasoned tomato sauce or ketchup and sprinkle with 2 tablespoons each grated Parmesan and shredded mozzarella cheeses; cover and cook until cheeses are melted, 5 to 10 minutes.

Savory Cheese Meat Loaf—Make recipe as above, substituting ½ pound (224 gm) ground lean pork for ½ pound (224 gm) of the beef, and adding 4 ounces (112 gm) cream cheese, ½ cup (2 ounces [56 gm]) shredded Cheddar cheese, and 2 tablespoons (30 mL) Worcestershire sauce. At the end of cooking time, sprinkle ¼ cup (1 ounce [28 gm]) shredded Cheddar cheese over top of meat loaf; cover and cook until cheese is melted, 5 to 10 minutes.

Chutney-Peanut Meat Loaf—Make recipe as above, substituting ½ cup (118 mL) chopped chutney for the ketchup, and adding ⅓ cup (79 mL) chopped peanuts, 1 teaspoon 92.5 mL) curry powder, and ¼ teaspoon (1.2 mL) ground ginger.

BRAISED SHORT RIBS >

You'll find these short ribs especially tasty and juicy—nibbling on the bones is allowed!

4 SERVINGS

INGREDIENTS

1 cup (236 mL) dry red wine or beef broth
4 large carrots, thickly sliced
1 large onion, cut into wedges
2 bay leaves
1 teaspoon (5 mL) dried marjoram
2 pounds (.91 kg) beef short ribs

1. Combine all ingredients in slow cooker, placing short ribs on the top; cover and cook on low 7 to 8 hours. Discard bay leaves.

SLOPPY JOES

A great sandwich for kids of all ages! Serve with lots of pickles and fresh vegetable relishes.

6–8 SERVINGS

INGREDIENTS

1 pound (454 gm) ground beef

1 cup (236 mL) each: chopped onion, green or red bell pepper

2 teaspoons (10 mL) minced garlic

l cup (236 mL) ketchup

½ cup (118 mL) water

¼ cup (59 mL) packed light brown sugar

2 tablespoons (30 mL) prepared mustard

2 teaspoons (10 mL) each: celery seeds, chili powder

Salt and pepper, to taste

6–8 whole-wheat hamburger buns, toasted

8 sweet or dill pickle spears

1. Cook ground beef in lightly greased skillet until browned, crumbling with a fork. Combine ground beef and remaining ingredients, except salt, pepper, buns, and pickles, in slow cooker; cover and cook on high 2 to 3 hours. Season to taste with salt and pepper. Serve in buns with pickles.

VARIATION

Vegetarian Joes—Make recipe as above, omitting ground beef; add 1 cup (236 mL) each textured vegetable protein and sliced mushrooms, and increase water to 1½ cups (354 mL).

CHEESEBURGER JOES

A cheeseburger deluxe, made sloppy Joe-style! Everyone will line up for this cheesy sandwich!

12 SERVINGS

INGREDIENTS

2 pounds (.91 kg) lean ground beef
¾ cup (177 mL) each: chopped onion, green bell pepper
8 ounces (224 gm) sliced mushrooms
1 tablespoon (15 mL) minced garlic
½ cup (118 mL) each: crumbled fried bacon, sweet pickle relish, yellow mustard
¾ cup (177 mL) ketchup
1 tablespoon (15 mL) Worcestershire sauce
8 ounces (224 gm) processed cheese, cubed
Salt and pepper, to taste
12 hamburger buns, toasted

1. Cook beef, onion, and bell pepper over medium heat in large skillet until beef is browned, crumbling with a fork; transfer to slow cooker. Add remaining ingredients, except salt, pepper, and buns; cover and cook on low 2 to 3 hours. Season to taste with salt and pepper; serve on buns.

ITALIAN BEEF SANDWICHES

Slow cooked to savory goodness!

12 SERVINGS

INGREDIENTS

1 boneless beef rump roast (about 3 pounds [1.36 kg])
3 cups (708 mL) beef broth
1 package (.7 ounce [20 gm]) Italian salad dressing mix
1 bay leaf
1 teaspoon (5 mL) pepper
12 buns or Italian rolls

1. Combine all ingredients, except buns, in slow cooker; cover and cook on low 10 to 12 hours. Remove meat and shred; return to slow cooker. Serve meat and juices in buns.

FRENCH DIP SANDWICHES

Tender beef, served in a bun, with flavorful broth for dipping—let guests make their own sandwiches.

12 SERVINGS

INGREDIENTS

1 boneless beef chuck roast (about 3 pounds [1.36 kg])
Pepper, to taste
2 cups (473 mL) beef broth
1 cup (236 mL) dry red wine or beef broth
1 package (1 ounce [28 gm]) onion soup mix
1 teaspoon (5 mL) minced garlic
12 hard rolls
6 ounces (170 gm) sliced provolone cheese

1. Sprinkle chuck roast lightly with pepper and place in slow cooker; add remaining ingredients, except rolls and cheese.

Cover and cook on low 6 to 8 hours. Remove chuck roast and slice thinly; return to slow cooker and turn heat to warm. Serve beef on hard rolls with provolone cheese; serve broth for dipping.

PHILLY CHEESE STEAK SANDWICHES

Sandwiches can be briefly put under the broiler to melt the cheese.

6–8 SERVINGS

INGREDIENTS

1 pound (454 gm) boneless round steak, thinly sliced
1 cup (136 mL) each: thinly sliced onion, green bell pepper, beef broth
1 teaspoon(5 mL) minced garlic
1 tablespoon (15 mL) Worcestershire sauce
Salt and pepper, to taste
6–8 hard or hoagie rolls
1–1½ cups (236–354 mL) (6 to 8 ounces [170–224 gm]) shredded mozzarella cheese

1. Combine all ingredients, except salt, pepper, rolls, and cheese, in slow cooker; cover and cook on low 6 to 8 hours. Season to taste with salt and pepper. Top rolls with meat and vegetable mixture; sprinkle with cheese. If desired, broil 6 inches from heat source until cheese is melted, 3 to 4 minutes.

PORK STEWS AND ENTRÉES

PORK, ARTICHOKE, AND WHITE BEAN STEW

An elegant and flavorful stew with Tuscan flavors.

6 ENTRÉE SERVINGS

INGREDIENTS

1½ pounds (681 gm) boneless pork loin, cubed (¾-inch)
1 can (14½ ounces [406 gm]) diced tomatoes, undrained
1 can (15 ounces [420 gm]) cannellini or navy beans,
   rinsed, drained
⅔ cup (158 mL) reduced-sodium fat-free chicken broth
2 cloves garlic, minced
1 teaspoon (5 mL) each: dried rosemary leaves, grated
   orange zest
1 can (14 ounces [392 gm]) artichoke hearts, rinsed,
   drained, quartered
1 tablespoon (5 mL) cornstarch
2 tablespoons (30 mL) cold water
Salt and pepper, to taste

1. Combine all ingredients, except artichokes, cornstarch, water, salt, and pepper, in slow cooker; cover and cook on low 6 to 8 hours, adding artichoke hearts during last 30 minutes. Turn heat to high and cook 10 minutes; stir in combined cornstarch and water, stirring 2 to 3 minutes. Season to taste with salt and pepper.

BARBECUE PORK STEW

Barbecue sauce and apple cider are the flavor secrets in this tasty stew.

4 ENTRÉE SERVINGS

INGREDIENTS

1 pound boneless pork loin, cubed (¾-inch [2 cm])
1½ (354 mL) cups apple cider or apple juice, divided
½ cup (118 mL) honey-mustard barbecue sauce
4 cups (.95 L) thinly sliced cabbage
1 medium onion, coarsely chopped
1 large tart apple, peeled, coarsely chopped
1 teaspoon (5 mL) crushed caraway seeds
1 tablespoon (15 mL) cornstarch
3 tablespoons (45 mL) cold water
Salt and pepper, to taste
8 ounces noodles, cooked, warm

1. Combine all ingredients, except cornstarch, water, salt, pepper, and noodles, in slow cooker; cover and cook on low 6 to 8 hours. Turn heat to high and cook 10 minutes; stir in combined cornstarch and water, stirring 2 to 3 minutes. Season to taste with salt and pepper; serve over noodles.

HERBED PORK CHOPS

Enjoy the convenience of canned soup in making these delectable pork chops.

4 SERVINGS

INGREDIENTS

4 boneless loin pork chops (4 ounces [112 gm] each)
1 teaspoon (5 mL) dried thyme leaves
Salt and pepper
1 small onion, halved, sliced
4 green onions, thinly sliced
1 small rib celery, sliced
1 can (10 ounces [280 gm]) cream of celery soup
½ cup (118 mL) 2% milk

1. Sprinkle pork chops with thyme, salt, and pepper; place in slow cooker, adding onions and celery. Pour combined soup and milk over; cover and cook on low 4 to 5 hours.

VARIATION

Portobello Pork Chops—Make recipe as above, omitting small onion and celery, adding 1 cup (236 mL) chopped portobello mushrooms, and substituting cream of mushroom soup for the celery soup.

PORK, POTATO, AND CABBAGE STEW

Serve this robust pork stew over noodles or rice.

4 ENTRÉE SERVINGS

INGREDIENTS

1 pound boneless lean pork loin
1 can (14½ ounces [406 gm]) stewed tomatoes, undrained
1 can (8 ounces [224 gm]) tomato sauce
2 cups (473 mL) each: thinly sliced cabbage, cubed peeled potatoes
1 large onion, finely chopped
2 cloves garlic, minced
1 tablespoon (15 mL) brown sugar
2 teaspoons (10 mL) each: balsamic vinegar, dried thyme leaves
1 bay leaf
Salt and pepper, to taste

1. Combine all ingredients, except salt and pepper, in slow cooker; cover and cook on low 6 to 8 hours. Discard bay leaf; season to taste with salt and pepper.

PORK LOIN WITH MUSTARD SAUCE

This pork loin cooks to perfect doneness in about 4 hours and can be carved at the dinner table. The mustard sauce is superb!

8 SERVINGS

INGREDIENTS

1 cup (236 mL) chopped onion
½ cup (118 mL) chicken broth
1 boneless pork loin roast (about 3 pounds [1.36 kg])
Paprika
Salt and pepper
Mustard Sauce (recipe follows)

1. Place onion and broth in slow cooker. Sprinkle pork lightly with paprika, salt, and pepper; insert meat thermometer in center of roast so tip is in center of meat. Place pork in slow cooker; cover and cook on low until meat thermometer registers 160°F (71°C), about 4 hours. Remove pork to serving platter and let stand, loosely covered with foil, 10 minutes. Strain broth and onions; spoon onions around pork. Reserve the broth for soup or another use. Serve pork with Mustard Sauce.

MUSTARD SAUCE

MAKES ABOUT 1½ CUPS (354 ML)

INGREDIENTS

1 cup (236 mL) sugar
¼ cup (59 mL) dry mustard
1 tablespoon (15 mL) all-purpose flour
½ cup (118 mL) cider vinegar
2 eggs
1 tablespoon (15 mL) margarine or butter

1. Mix sugar, dry mustard, and flour in small saucepan; whisk in vinegar and eggs. Cook over low heat until thickened, about 10 minutes; stir in margarine.

VARIATIONS

Roast Pork with Marmalade Sauce—Make recipe above, omitting onion and Mustard Sauce; reserve broth for soup or another use. To make *Marmalade Sauce*: Heat 1½ cups (354 mL) orange marmalade, 2 tablespoons (30 mL) margarine and 2 tablespoons (30 mL) orange liqueur or water in small saucepan until hot; serve with pork.

Pork Loin with Onion Gravy—Make recipe as above, omitting Mustard Sauce. Measure broth mixture and heat to boiling in medium saucepan. For each cup broth mixture, stir in combined 2 tablespoons (30 mL) flour combined with ¼ cup (59 mL) cold water or half-and-half, stirring until thickened, about 1 minute. Season to taste with salt and pepper; serve gravy with pork.

Pork Loin with Gingered Tomato Relish—Make recipe as above, omitting Mustard Sauce. Strain broth mixture, reserving broth for soup or another use. To make *Gingered Tomato Relish*: Heat reserved onions, 1½ cups (354 mL) chopped tomato, ½ cup (118 mL) each finely chopped zucchini and carrot, and 1 tablespoon (15 mL) minced gingerroot in medium skillet, covered, over medium-high heat until tomatoes are soft and mixture is bubbly, 3 to 4 minutes. Simmer rapidly, uncovered, until excess liquid is gone, about 5 minutes. Season to taste with salt and pepper; serve relish with pork.

Pork Loin with Cranberry Coulis—Make recipe as above, omitting Mustard Sauce and onion and reserving broth for soup or another use. To make *Cranberry Coulis*, heat 1½ cups (354 mL) fresh or frozen cranberries, 1 cup (236 mL) orange juice, ¼ cup (59 mL) sugar and 2–3 tablespoons (30–45 mL) honey to boiling in medium saucepan; reduce heat and simmer, covered, until cranberries are tender, 5 to 8 minutes. Process in food processor or blender until almost smooth. Serve coulis with pork.

PULLED PORK SANDWICHES, SOUTHERN-STYLE >

White Barbecue Sauce is popular in the South; these sandwiches can be served either on biscuits or small buns.

12 SERVINGS

INGREDIENTS

1 boneless pork loin roast (about 2 pounds [1.1 L])
Brown Sugar Rub (recipe follows)
½ cup (118 mL) chicken broth
12 biscuits or small buns
White Barbecue Sauce (recipe follows)

1. Rub pork loin with Brown Sugar Rub; place in slow cooker with broth. Cover and cook on low 6 to 8 hours. Remove pork and shred; reserve cooking liquid for soup or another use.

2. Spoon meat onto bottoms of biscuits and top with White Barbecue Sauce and biscuit tops.

BROWN SUGAR RUB

MAKES ABOUT ¼ CUP (59 ML)

INGREDIENTS

¼ cup (59 mL) packed light brown sugar
1 teaspoon (5 mL) garlic powder
½ teaspoon (2.5 mL) each: ground cumin, salt, pepper

1. Mix all ingredients.

WHITE BARBECUE SAUCE

MAKES ABOUT 2½ CUPS (591 ML)

INGREDIENTS
1½ (354 mL) cups mayonnaise
¼ cup (59 mL) apple cider vinegar
1 tablespoon (15 mL) sugar
1 clove garlic, minced
2 teaspoons (10 mL) horseradish (optional)
1–2 tablespoons (15–30 mL) lemon juice

1. Mix all ingredients, adding lemon juice to taste.

PICADILLO TACOS

These soft tacos are perfect party fare!

6 SERVINGS

INGREDIENTS
12 ounces (340 gm) pork tenderloin
¼ cup (59 mL) each: water, thinly sliced green onion
1 teaspoon (5 mL) each: minced garlic, jalapeño pepper,
　ground cinnamon
¼ teaspoon (1.2 mL) dried oregano leaves
1–2 teaspoons (5–10 mL) cider vinegar
¼ cup (59 mL) each: raisins, slivered almonds
Salt and pepper, to taste
6 flour tortillas (6-inch [15 cm]), warm
¾ cup (177 mL) each: chopped tomato, avocado
Cilantro sprigs, for garnish
Salsa, for serving

1. Combine pork, water, green onion, garlic, jalapeño pepper, cinnamon, oregano, and vinegar in slow cooker; cover and cook on low 3 hours. Remove pork and shred with 2 forks; return to slow cooker; add raisins and almonds. Cover and cook on low 1 hour; season to taste with salt and pepper.

2. Top each tortilla with about ¼ cup (59 mL) pork mixture; sprinkle with 1 tablespoon (15 mL) each tomato and avocado and several sprigs cilantro. Roll up and serve with salsa.

CHICKEN STEWS AND ENTRÉES

SWEET POTATO CHICKEN STEW

The stew is also delicious made with russet potatoes, or a combination of russet and sweet potatoes.

4 ENTRÉE SERVINGS

INGREDIENTS

1 pound (454 gm) boneless, skinless chicken breast, cubed (1-inch [2.5 cm])
1½ cups (354 mL) reduced-sodium fat-free chicken broth
12 ounces (340 mL) sweet potatoes, cubed (¾-inch [2 cm])
1 large green bell pepper, sliced
2–3 teaspoons (10–15 mL) chili powder
½ teaspoon (2.5 mL) garlic powder
2 tablespoons (30 mL) cornstarch
¼ cup (59 mL) cold water
Salt and pepper, to taste

1. Combine all ingredients, except cornstarch, water, salt, and pepper, in slow cooker; cover and cook on high 4 to 5 hours. Stir in combined cornstarch and water, stirring 2 to 3 minutes. Season to taste with salt and pepper.

CHICKEN AND MUSHROOM STEW

Serve this stew with warm slices of bread.

4 ENTRÉE SERVINGS

INGREDIENTS

1 pound (454 gm) boneless, skinless chicken breast, cubed
   (¾-inch [2 cm])
1 cup reduced-sodium fat-free chicken broth
1 can (6 ounces [170 gm]) tomato paste
1 tablespoon (15 mL) Worcestershire sauce
8 ounces (224 gm) mushrooms, thickly sliced
1 large onion, chopped
2 each: minced cloves garlic, coarsely shredded large carrots
1 bay leaf
1 teaspoon dried Italian seasoning
¼ teaspoon (1.25 mL) dry mustard
1–2 tablespoons (15–30 mL) cornstarch
2–4 tablespoons (30–60 mL) cold water
Salt and pepper, to taste
2 cups rice, cooked, warm

1. Combine all ingredients, except cornstarch, water, salt, pepper, and rice, in slow cooker; cover and cook on high 4 to 6 hours. Stir in combined cornstarch and water, stirring 2 to 3 minutes. Discard bay leaf; season to taste with salt. Serve over rice.

LEMON CHICKEN STEW

Fresh lemon juice and jalapeño pepper are the flavor accents in this delicious stew.

6 ENTRÉE SERVINGS

INGREDIENTS

1 pound (454 gm) boneless, skinless chicken breast, cubed
2 cans (14½ ounces [406 gm] each) diced tomatoes, undrained
1 jalapeño pepper, minced
2 cloves garlic, minced
1 teaspoon (5 mL) instant chicken bouillon crystals
2 teaspoons (10 mL) dried basil leaves
2 cups (473 mL) broccoli florets
¼–⅓ cup (59–79 mL) lemon juice
Salt and pepper, to taste
12 ounces (340 gm) angel hair pasta, cooked, warm
Shredded Parmesan cheese, for garnish

1. Combine all ingredients, except broccoli, lemon juice, salt, pepper, pasta, and cheese, in slow cooker; cover and cook on high 4 to 5 hours, adding broccoli during last 20 minutes. Season to taste with lemon juice, salt, and pepper. Serve over pasta; sprinkle with Parmesan cheese.

GINGER-ORANGE CHICKEN AND SQUASH STEW

Any winter squash, such as acorn, butternut, or hubbard, is a good choice for this orange and ginger-accented stew; sweet potatoes can be used too.

6 ENTRÉE SERVINGS

INGREDIENTS

1½ pounds (681 gm) boneless, skinless chicken breast, cubed

1 cup (236 mL) reduced-sodium fat-free chicken broth

1 can (14½ ounces [406 gm]) diced tomatoes, undrained

½ cup (118 mL) orange juice

3 cups (708 mL) peeled cubed winter yellow squash

2 medium Idaho potatoes, peeled, cubed

¾ cup (177 mL) each: coarsely chopped onion, green bell pepper

2 cloves garlic, minced

1 tablespoon (15 mL) grated orange zest

½ teaspoon (2.5 mL) ground ginger

½ cup (118 mL) reduced-fat sour cream

1 tablespoon (15 mL) cornstarch

Salt and pepper, to taste

4 cups cooked noodles or brown basmati rice, warm

1. Combine all ingredients, except sour cream, cornstarch, salt, pepper, and noodles, in 6-quart slow cooker; cover and cook on low 6 to 8 hours. Stir in combined sour cream and cornstarch, stirring 2 to 3 minutes. Season to taste with salt and pepper. Serve over noodles.

ROAST CHICKEN WITH CRANBERRY-ORANGE RELISH >

Using a meat thermometer assures that the chicken will be cooked to the correct doneness for perfect slicing. The Cranberry-Orange Relish recipe makes an ample amount; it can be made in advance and refrigerated for several weeks, but be sure to make it at least a day in advance and chill overnight. After all, you'll need your slow cooker free for the chicken!

6 SERVINGS

INGREDIENTS

1 whole chicken (about 3 pounds [1.36 kg])
Paprika
Salt and pepper
½ cup (118 mL) chicken broth
1½ cups (354 mL) Cranberry-Orange Relish (recipe follows)

1. Make foil handles (see p. 23) and fit into slow cooker. Sprinkle chicken lightly with paprika, salt, and pepper; insert meat thermometer so tip is in thickest part of inside thigh, not touching bone. Place chicken in slow cooker; add broth. Cover and cook on low until thermometer registers 175°F (80°C), 4 to 5 hours. Remove chicken, using foil handles; place on serving platter and cover loosely with foil. Reserve broth for soup or another use. Serve chicken with Cranberry-Orange Relish.

CRANBERRY-ORANGE RELISH

MAKES ABOUT 4 CUPS (.95 L)

INGREDIENTS

5 large navel oranges
1 cup (236 mL) water
3 cups (708 mL) sugar
1 package (12 ounces [340 gm]) cranberries
½ cup (118 mL) coarsely chopped walnuts

1. Grate zest from 3 oranges; reserve. Peel oranges and cut into sections. Combine all ingredients in slow cooker; cover and cook on low 6 to 7 hours. If thicker consistency is desired, cook uncovered until thickened. Chill overnight.

ROAST CHICKEN WITH MASHED POTATOES AND GRAVY

You'll never taste a more delicious, moist, perfectly cooked chicken!

6 SERVINGS

INGREDIENTS
1 whole chicken (about 3 pounds [1.36 kg])
Paprika
Salt and pepper
½ cup (118 mL) chicken broth or water
¼ cup (59 mL) all-purpose flour
½ cup (118 mL) cold water
Salt and pepper, to taste
Real Mashed Potatoes (see recipe p. 104)

1. Make foil handles (see p. 23) and fit into slow cooker. Sprinkle chicken lightly with paprika, salt, and pepper; insert meat thermometer so tip is in thickest part of inside thigh, not touching bone. Place chicken in slow cooker; add broth. Cover and cook on low until thermometer registers 175°F (80°C), 4 to 5 hours. Remove chicken, using foil handles; place on serving platter and cover loosely with foil.

2. Pour broth into measuring cup; spoon off fat. Measure 2 cups broth into small saucepan and heat to boiling. Whisk in combined flour and water, whisking until thickened, about 1 minute. Season to taste with salt and pepper. Serve chicken with Real Mashed Potatoes and gravy.

INDONESIAN CHICKEN WITH ZUCCHINI

You'll enjoy the subtle blending of coconut milk, gingerroot, garlic, cilantro, and cumin in this dish.

6 SERVINGS

INGREDIENTS

6 large skinless chicken breast halves (6–8 ounces [170–340 gm] each)
1 can (15 ounces [425 gm]) light coconut milk
¼ cup (59 mL) each: water, lemon juice
1 medium onion, finely chopped
1 clove garlic, minced
3 tablespoons (45 mL) minced gingerroot or 2 teaspoons (10 mL) ground ginger
2 teaspoons (10 mL) ground coriander
1 teaspoon (5 mL) ground cumin
1 pound (454 gm) zucchini, halved lengthwise, seeded, sliced
1 tablespoon (15 mL) cornstarch
2 tablespoons (30 mL) water
⅓ cup (79 mL) chopped cilantro
Salt and pepper, to taste
4 cups (.95 L) cooked rice, warm

1. Place all ingredients, except zucchini, cornstarch, 2 tablespoons (30 mL) water, cilantro, salt, pepper, and rice, in slow cooker; cover and cook on low 3½ to 4 hours, adding zucchini during last 30 minutes. Remove chicken breasts and keep warm. Turn heat to high and cook 10 minutes; stir in combined cornstarch and 2 tablespoons (30 mL) water, stirring 2 to 3 minutes. Stir in cilantro; season to taste with salt and pepper. Serve chicken and broth over rice in shallow bowls.

SHERRIED CHICKEN

A lovely dish for entertaining or for special family meals. Serve over an aromatic rice to absorb flavorful juices.

4 SERVINGS

INGREDIENTS

¼ cup (59 mL) dry sherry
1 cup golden raisins
4 skinless chicken breast halves (about 6 ounces [170 gm] each)
½ cup (118 mL) coarsely chopped walnuts
1 tart cooking apple, peeled, chopped
1 small red onion, sliced
2 cloves garlic, minced
1 cup (236 mL) chicken broth
Salt and pepper, to taste

1. Pour sherry over raisins in bowl; let stand 15 to 30 minutes. Place all ingredients, except salt and pepper, in slow cooker; cover and cook on high until chicken is tender, 3 to 4 hours. Season to taste with salt and pepper.

CHICKEN MOLE

This easy Mole Sauce is made with canned chili beans!

4 SERVINGS

INGREDIENTS

Mole Sauce (recipe follows)
4 skinless chicken breast halves (about 4 ounces [112 gm] each)
3 cups (708 mL) cooked rice, warm
Chopped cilantro, for garnish
½ cup (118 mL) sour cream

1. Spoon 1 cup Mole Sauce into slow cooker; top with chicken breasts and remaining sauce. Cover and cook on low 4 to 6 hours. Serve over rice; sprinkle generously with cilantro and serve with sour cream.

MOLE SAUCE

MAKES ABOUT 2½ CUPS (591 ML)

INGREDIENTS

1 can (15 ounces [425 gm]) beans in hot chili sauce, undrained
½ cup (118 mL) coarsely chopped onion
2 cloves garlic
¼ cup (59 mL) tomato sauce
1 tablespoon (15 mL) Worcestershire sauce
½ teaspoon (2.5 mL) ground cinnamon
½ ounce (14 gm) unsweetened chocolate, finely chopped
¼ cup (59 mL) slivered almonds

1. Process all ingredients in food processor until smooth.

BUTTER CHICKEN

If you make this dish and wonder why it doesn't really look like the butter chicken you eat in most restaurants, congratulations, you've made it correctly! Most mainstream Indian restaurants serve tandoori chicken smothered in butter and cream as a poor substitute.

GS

INGREDIENTS

8 tablespoons (118 mL) ghee or unsalted butter
4 pounds (2 kg) boneless, skinless chicken breasts and/or thighs
1 (4-inch [10 cm]) piece fresh gingerroot, peeled and chopped into 1-inch (2.5 cm) cubes
8 cloves garlic, peeled
1 cup (236 g) blanched sliced almonds
½ cup (118 mL) water
2 large onions, peeled and thinly sliced
1½ cups (354 mL) plain yogurt
2 teaspoons (10 mL) each: red chili powder, garam masala
1 teaspoon (5 mL) each: ground cloves, ground cinnamon
8 green cardamom pods, lightly crushed in a mortar and pestle
2 tablespoons (30 mL) salt
5 medium tomatoes, chopped
½–1 cup (118–236 g) chopped fresh cilantro
½ cup (118 mL) heavy cream or half-and-half
Chopped onions, for garnish
Chopped green chili peppers, for garnish
Basmati rice, cooked, warm, for serving

1. Turn slow cooker to high and add the ghee. Heat for 20 to 25 minutes, until it melts.

2. Meanwhile, cut chicken into 2½-inch (7 cm) strips. Set aside.

3. Process gingerroot, garlic, and almonds in food processor until smooth. Add water and process to a thick, almost creamy paste. Set aside.

4. Add onions to slow cooker and lightly fry 15 minutes, stirring once or twice until soft and lightly brown.

5. Meanwhile, whisk together gingerroot mixture, yogurt, red chili powder, garam masala, cloves, cinnamon, cardamom, and salt in large bowl. Fold in the tomatoes. Pour over the chicken ix-ing well. Turn slow cooker to low and add the chicken. ⌐ and cook for 6 hours.

6. Stir cilantro and cream into chicken mixture. Garnish w chopped onions and green chili peppers. Serve with basn

CHICKEN CURRY

When most people think of Indian food, the first dish that comes to mind is a good chicken curry.

6 ENTRÉE SERVINGS

INGREDIENTS
3 pounds (1.36 kg) skinless whole chicken, cut in about 8 pieces (boneless chicken pieces can also be used)
1 large yellow or red onion, cut into 8 pieces
2 medium tomatoes, quartered
1 (4-inch [10 cm]) piece gingerroot, cut into 1-inch (2.5 cm) pieces
10 cloves garlic
1 tablespoon (15 mL) each: salt, turmeric, garam masala
¼ cup (59 mL) vegetable or canola oil
1 cup (236 mL) plain yogurt
1 tablespoon (15 mL) red chili powder
1 cup (236 mL) dried methi leaves (dried fenugreek leaves)
1 (2–4 inch [5–10 cm]) cinnamon stick
4 green cardamom pods
4 cloves
4–6 green Thai or Serrano chiles, or cayenne peppers, stems removed, halved lengthwise
½ cup (118 mL) boiling water (optional)
Basmati or brown rice, cooked, warm
½ cup (100 g) fresh cilantro, chopped, for garnish

1. Place chicken in the slow cooker.

2. Process onion, tomatoes, gingerroot, and garlic until smooth. Transfer paste to a bowl. Whisk in the salt, turmeric, garam masala, oil, yogurt, red chili powder, and methi. Pour over the chicken.

3. Add cinnamon stick, cardamom pods, cloves, and green chili peppers, mixing gently; cover and cook on low 8 hours. For more brothy curry, add boiling water during the last 30 minutes of cooking, if desired. Discard whole spices. Serve over rice and garnish with cilantro.

CHICKEN DIVAN >

This rich, sherry-laced sauce nicely complements tender chicken breasts. This recipe comes from Sue Spitler, author of 1,001 Best Slow-Cooker Recipes.

6 ENTRÉE SERVINGS

INGREDIENTS

Sauce Divan (recipe follows)
6 boneless, skinless chicken breast halves (3 to 4 ounces [85–112 gm] each), halved
3 cups (708 mL) broccoli florets and sliced stems
4 cups (.95 L) cooked brown rice, warm
Grated Parmesan cheese, for garnish
Paprika, for garnish

1. Spoon 1 cup (236 mL) Sauce Divan into slow cooker; top with chicken and remaining sauce. Cover and cook on low 4 to 5 hours, stirring in broccoli during last 30 minutes. Serve over rice; sprinkle with Parmesan cheese and paprika.

SAUCE DIVAN

INGREDIENTS

3 tablespoons (15 mL) margarine or butter
¼ cup (59 mL) all-purpose flour
2½ cups (591 mL) half-and-half or light cream
¼ cup (59 mL) dry sherry or half-and-half
Salt and pepper, to taste

1. Melt margarine in medium saucepan; stir in flour and cook 1 to 2 minutes. Whisk in half-and-half and heat to boiling, whisking until thickened, about 1 minute. Whisk in sherry; season to taste with salt and pepper.

PULLED CHICKEN SANDWICHES

Friends will ask for this tangy barbecue recipe!

8 ENTRÉE SERVINGS

INGREDIENTS

1 pound boneless, skinless chicken breasts, quartered
1 can (12 ounces [340 gm]) cola
1 cup (236 mL) ketchup
⅓ cup (79 mL) yellow mustard
¼ cup (59 mL) packed light brown sugar
½ cup (118 mL) chopped onion
1 teaspoon (5 mL) minced garlic
2 tablespoons (30 mL) cornstarch
¼ cup (59 mL) cold water
Salt and pepper, to taste
8 hamburger buns

1. Combine all ingredients, except cornstarch, water, salt, pepper, and buns, in slow cooker; cover and cook on low 6 to 8 hours. Turn heat to high and cook 10 minutes; stir in combined cornstarch and cold water, stirring 2 to 3 minutes. Stir to shred chicken; season to taste with salt and pepper. Serve in buns.

LAMB STEWS AND ENTRÉES

IRISH LAMB STEW

An Irish comfort food, this simply seasoned stew is always welcome on cold winter evenings.

6 ENTRÉE SERVINGS

INGREDIENTS

1½ pounds (681 gm) lamb cubes for stew
2 cups (473 mL) chicken broth
2 medium onions, sliced
6 each: quartered medium potatoes, thickly sliced medium carrots
½ teaspoon (2.5 mL) dried thyme leaves
1 bay leaf
½ cup (118 mL) frozen peas, thawed
2 tablespoons (30 mL) cornstarch
¼ cup (59 mL) cold water
1–1½ teaspoons (5–7.5 mL) Worcestershire sauce
Salt and pepper, to taste

1. Combine all ingredients, except peas, cornstarch, water, Worcestershire sauce, salt, and pepper, in slow cooker; cover and cook on low 6 to 8 hours. Add peas, turn heat to high and cook 10 minutes; stir in combined cornstarch and water, stirring 2 to 3 minutes. Discard bay leaf; season to taste with Worcestershire sauce, salt, and pepper.

SAVORY LAMB STEW

Enjoy this rich and flavorful combination of lamb shanks, lentils, vegetables, and spices.

6 ENTRÉE SERVINGS

INGREDIENTS

2 pounds (.91 kg) lamb shanks, fat trimmed
1½ cups (354 mL) chicken broth
1 can (14½ ounces [406 gm]) diced tomatoes, undrained
½ cup (118 mL) each: brown dried lentils, sliced carrots, chopped green bell pepper
2 cups (473 mL) chopped onions
2 cloves garlic, minced
2 bay leaves
2 teaspoons (10 mL) dried thyme leaves
¼ teaspoon (1.25 mL) each: ground cinnamon and cloves
Salt and pepper, to taste
1¼ cups (265 mL) cooked brown rice, warm

1. Combine all ingredients, except salt, pepper, and rice, in 6-quart slow cooker; cover and cook on low 6 to 8 hours. Discard bay leaves. Remove lamb shanks; remove lean meat and cut into bite-sized pieces. Return meat to stew; season to taste with salt and pepper. Serve over rice.

LAMB BIRYANI

The combination of rice, lamb, and vegetables makes this a comforting, delicious, and convenient dish. This recipe comes from Anupy Singla, author of The Indian Slow Cooker.

4 ENTRÉE SERVINGS

INGREDIENTS

1 (4-inch [10-cm]) piece gingerroot, grated
4 garlic cloves, grated
4–6 green Thai or Serrano chiles, or cayenne peppers, stems removed
2 tablespoons (30 mL) garam masala
1 teaspoon (5 mL) each: red chili powder, turmeric powder, salt
⅔ cup (160 g) chopped cilantro
¼ cup (50 gm) mint, chopped
2 pounds (.91 kg) boneless lamb leg or shoulder, cubed (1-inch [2.5 cm])
1 cup (236 mL) plain yogurt
3 medium yellow or red onions, very thinly sliced
4 tablespoons (59 mL) canola or vegetable oil, divided
1½ cups (354 mL) water
2½ cups (526 gm) uncooked basmati rice
1 tablespoon (15 mL) salt
½ teaspoon (2.5 mL) saffron strands, soaked in 2 table-spoons (30 mL) milk (optional)

1. Combine ginger, garlic, green chiles, garam masala, red chili powder, turmeric, salt, cilantro, and mint in large bowl. Add lamb, mixing to coat. Refrigerated at least 2 hours or, ideally, overnight.

2. Stir yogurt into lamb mixture.

3. Combine onions, 2 tablespoons (30 mL) oil, and lamb mixture in slow cooker. Cover and cook 2 hours.

4. Heat water to boiling in medium saucepan over medium-high heat. Add rice and salt; simmer over low heat 3 to 5 minutes, until most of the water has evaporated. Using a slotted spoon, transfer the rice to slow cooker, discarding any remaining water. Level rice with back of a spoon. Drizzle with remaining 2 tablespoons (30 mL) oil and saffron mixture, if desired.

5. Cover and cook 1 hour, mixing once or twice.

MINCED LAMB WITH PEAS

Follow this recipe, and your guests will think you slaved over a hot stove all day long!

8 ENTRÉE SERVINGS

INGREDIENTS

4 pounds (2 kg) minced lamb
½ cup (118 mL) vegetable or canola oil
1 yellow or red onion, roughly chopped
1 (4-inch [10 cm]) piece gingerroot, cubed
20 cloves garlic
10 green Thai or Serrano chiles, or cayenne peppers, stems removed
1 (16-ounce [454 gm]) can tomato puree
8 fresh or dried Indian or regular bay leaves
4 tablespoons (59 mL) each: ground cumin, coriander
2 tablespoons (30 mL) each: garam masala, red chili powder, salt
1 teaspoon (5 mL) ground turmeric
½ cup (100 gm) chopped cilantro
2 cups (402 gm) fresh or frozen peas
Basmati rice, cooked, warm
Sliced green onions, for serving

1. Combine lamb and oil in slow cooker. Heat on low while you prep the other ingredients.

2. Process onion, ginger, garlic, and green chilies in food processor until smooth. Add to slow cooker with tomato puree, bay leaves, cumin, coriander, garam masala, red chili powder, salt, and turmeric.

3. Cover and cook on high 7 hours. Discard bay leaves. Turn slow cooker off and add cilantro and peas. (If peas are fresh, cook them in boiling water for about 3 minutes before adding.) Cover and let stand 10 minutes.

4. Serve with rice and green onions.

HEARTY ROSEMARY LAMB STEW WITH SWEET POTATOES >

The pairing of rosemary and lamb is classic, distinctive, and delightful.

4 ENTRÉE SERVINGS

INGREDIENTS
1 pound (454 gm) boneless lamb shoulder, fat trimmed, cubed (¾-inch)
1½ cups (681 mL) beef broth
1 pound (454 gm) sweet potatoes, peeled, cubed (¾-inch)
1½ cups (354 mL) cut green beans
1 large onion, cut into thin wedges
1 teaspoon (5 mL) dried rosemary leaves
2 bay leaves
1–2 tablespoons (15–30 mL) cornstarch
¼ cup (59 mL) cold water
Salt and pepper, to taste

1. Combine all ingredients, except cornstarch, water, salt, and pepper, in slow cooker; cover and cook on low 6 to 8 hours. Turn heat to high and cook 10 minutes; stir in combined cornstarch and water, stirring 2 to 3 minutes. Discard bay leaves; season to taste with salt and pepper.

GREEK PITAS

Ground beef, or a mixture of lamb and beef, can be used in these fla-vorful meatballs.

4 SERVINGS

INGREDIENTS

1 pound (454 gm) ground lamb
¾ cup (177 mL) fresh bread crumbs
1 egg
¼ cup (59 mL) finely chopped onion
1 teaspoon (5 mL) each: dried oregano and mint leaves
¾ teaspoon (3.7 mL) salt
½ teaspoon (5 mL) pepper
¾ cup (177 mL) chicken broth
2 pita breads, halved
Cucumber-Yogurt Sauce (recipe follows)
4 tablespoons crumbled feta cheese

1. Combine lamb, bread crumbs, egg, onion, oregano, mint, salt and pepper; shape into 16 meatballs. Place in slow cooker with chicken broth; cover and cook on low 4 hours. Drain and discard juices, or save for another use.

2. Spoon 4 meatballs into each pita half; top meatballs in each pita half with 2 tablespoons Cucumber-Yogurt sauce and 1 tablespoon (15 mL) feta cheese.

CUCUMBER-YOGURT SAUCE

MAKES ABOUT ½ CUP (118 ML)

INGREDIENTS

¼ cup (59 mL) each: plain yogurt, finely chopped seeded cucumber
1 teaspoon (5 mL) dried mint leaves

1. Mix all ingredients.

SEAFOOD STEWS AND ENTRÉES

CREOLE FISH STEW

Rich flavors and easy preparation—who could ask for more?

4 ENTRÉE SERVINGS

INGREDIENTS

1 can (28 ounces [284 kg]) diced tomatoes, undrained
¼ cup (59 mL) dry white wine or water
2 cups (473 mL) chopped onions
1 cup (236 mL) each: chopped green bell pepper, celery
½ teaspoon (2.5 mL) dried thyme leaves
⅛–¼ teaspoon (.6–1.25 mL) crushed red pepper
2 teaspoons (10 mL) minced garlic
2 tablespoons (30 mL) soy sauce
1 tablespoon (15 mL) paprika
2 bay leaves
1 pound (454 gm) cod fillets, cubed
Salt and pepper, to taste
3 cups (708 mL) rice, cooked, warm

1. Combine all ingredients, except cod, salt, pepper, and rice, in slow cooker; cover and cook on high 4 to 5 hours, adding cod during last 10 to 15 minutes. Discard bay leaves; season to taste with salt and pepper; serve over rice.

CARIBBEAN SWEET-SOUR SALMON STEW

Sweet and sour flavors team with salmon, pineapple, and black beans in this island-inspired stew.

4 ENTRÉE SERVINGS

INGREDIENTS

1 can (15 ounces [425 gm]) black beans, rinsed, drained
1 can (8 ounces [224 gm]) pineapple tidbits in juice, und-rained
1 cup (236 mL) each: coarsely chopped onion, sliced red and green bell peppers
4 cloves garlic, minced
2 teaspoons (10 mL) minced gingerroot
1 jalapeño pepper, finely chopped
2–3 tablespoons (30–45 mL) each: light brown sugar, cider vinegar
2–3 teaspoons (10–15 mL) curry powder
¼ cup (59 mL) cold water
1½ tablespoons (22.5 mL) cornstarch
1 pound (454 gm) salmon steaks, cubed (1½-inch [3.5 cm])
Salt and pepper, to taste
4 cups (.95 L) cooked rice, warm

1. Combine all ingredients, except water, cornstarch, salmon, salt, pepper, and rice, in slow cooker; cover and cook on high 4 to 5 hours. Stir in combined water and cornstarch, stirring 2 to 3 minutes. Add salmon; cook 10 to 15 minutes. Season to taste with salt and pepper. Serve over rice.

CIOPPINO WITH PASTA >

A California favorite! Substitute other kinds of fresh fish, according to availability and price.

6 ENTRÉE SERVINGS

INGREDIENTS

½ cup (118 mL) each: clam juice, dry white wine or clam juice

3 cups (708 mL) chopped tomatoes

1 cup (236 mL) each: chopped green bell pepper, onion, sliced mushrooms

4 cloves garlic, minced

1 tablespoon (15 mL) tomato paste

2 teaspoons (10 mL) each: dried oregano and basil leaves

1 teaspoon (5 mL) ground turmeric

1 pound (448 gm) sea scallops

4 ounces (112 gm) halibut or haddock steak, cubed (1-inch [2.5 cm])

12 mussels, scrubbed

Salt and pepper, to taste

12 ounces (340 gm) fettuccine, cooked, warm

1. Combine all ingredients, except seafood, salt, pepper, and fettuccine, in 6-quart slow cooker; cover and cook on low 6 to 8 hours, adding seafood during last 15 minutes. Discard any mussels that have not opened; season to taste with salt and pepper. Serve over fettuccine.

FISH STEW MARSALA

Marsala wine adds a distinctive, appealing note to this simple Italian fish stew.

4 ENTRÉE SERVINGS

INGREDIENTS

2½ cups (591 mL) reduced-sodium fat-free chicken broth
⅓ cup (79 mL) dry Marsala wine or chicken broth
¼ cup (59 mL) tomato paste
1 cup (236 mL) each: chopped onion, red and green bell peppers
½ cup (118 mL) chopped celery
1 teaspoon (5 mL) minced garlic
1 teaspoon (5 mL) dried thyme leaves
1 pound(454 gm) haddock steaks, cubed (2-inch)
2 cups (473 mL) cooked medium pasta shells, warm
2–3 tablespoons (30–45 mL) lemon juice
Salt and pepper, to taste

1. Combine all ingredients, except fish, pasta, lemon juice, salt, and pepper, in slow cooker; cover and cook on high 4 to 5 hours, adding fish and pasta during last 10 to 15 minutes. Season to taste with lemon juice, salt and pepper.

SCALLOP STEW, ITALIAN-STYLE

Scallops are a great addition to this easy, healthy stew.

4 ENTRÉE SERVINGS

INGREDIENTS

1 can (14½ ounces [406 gm]) Italian-style plum tomatoes, undrained, chopped

1 cup (236 mL) reduced-sodium fat-free chicken broth

1 each: chopped medium onion, medium green bell pepper, minced clove garlic

1 bay leaf

1 teaspoon (5 mL) dried basil leaves

2 cups (473 mL) small broccoli florets

12–16 ounces (340-454 gm) bay or sea scallops

2 teaspoons (10 mL) cornstarch

¼ cup (59 mL) cold water

2–4 tablespoons (30-60 mL) cup dry sherry (optional)

Salt and pepper, to taste

1 cup (236 mL) white or brown rice, cooked, warm

1. Combine tomatoes with liquid, broth, onion, bell pepper, garlic, bay leaf and basil in slow cooker; cover and cook on high 4 to 5 hours, adding broccoli during last 30 minutes and scallops during last 5 to 10 minutes. Stir in combined cornstarch and water, stirring 2 to 3 minutes. Discard bay leaf and season to taste with sherry, salt, and pepper. Serve over rice.

THAI-STYLE SHRIMP STEW >

Chinese chili sauce is HOT, so use it cautiously!

4 ENTRÉE SERVINGS

INGREDIENTS

2 cups (473 mL) each: reduced-sodium fat-free chicken broth, chopped bok choy

1 cup (236 mL) each: sliced red bell pepper, sliced scallions, fresh or canned rinsed drained bean sprouts

4 ounces (112 gm) bean threads or cellophane noodles, cut (2-inch)

¼ cup (59 mL) rice wine vinegar

½–1 teaspoon (2.5-5 mL) Chinese chili sauce with garlic

1 pound (454 gm) medium shrimp, peeled, deveined

Soy sauce, to taste

Salt and pepper, to taste

1. Combine broth, bok choy, bell pepper, scallions, and bean sprouts in slow cooker; cover and cook on high 4 to 5 hours.

2. While stew is cooking, soak cellophane noodles in hot water until softened; drain. Add noodles, vinegar, chili sauce, and shrimp to slow cooker during last 10 minutes. Season to taste with soy sauce, salt, and pepper.

POACHED SALMON WITH LEMON-CAPER SAUCE

Slow cooking gives the salmon extra moistness.

MAKES 4 SERVINGS

INGREDIENTS

½ cup (118 mL) each: water, dry white wine
1 thin slice yellow onion
1 bay leaf
½ teaspoon (2.5 mL) salt
4 salmon steaks (about 4 ounces [112 gm] each)
Lemon-Caper Sauce (recipe follows)

1. Combine water and wine in slow cooker; cover and cook on high 20 minutes. Add onion, bay leaf, salt, and salmon; cover and cook on high until salmon is tender and flakes with a fork, about 20 minutes. Discard bay leaf. Serve with Lemon-Caper Sauce.

LEMON-CAPER SAUCE

INGREDIENTS

2–3 tablespoons (30-45 mL) margarine or butter
3 tablespoons (45 mL) all-purpose flour
1 can (14½ ounces [406 gm]) chicken broth
2–3 teaspoons (10-15 mL) lemon juice
3 tablespoons (45 mL) capers
¼ teaspoon (1.25 mL) salt
⅛ teaspoon (.6 mL) white pepper

1. Melt margarine in small saucepan; stir in flour and cook over medium heat 1 minute. Whisk in chicken broth and lemon juice; heat to boiling, whisking until thickened, about 1 minute. Stir in capers, salt, and white pepper.

RED SNAPPER WITH GARLIC SAUCE

This garlic sauce is equally delicious with firm-fleshed white fish, such as halibut or haddock.

4 SERVINGS

INGREDIENTS

1 red snapper fillet (about 1¼ pounds [566 gm])
Salt and pepper
¼–½ cup (59-118 mL) clam juice or vegetable broth
Caramelized Garlic Sauce (recipe follows)

1. Line slow cooker with aluminum foil or make foil handles (see p. 23). Sprinkle fish lightly with salt and pepper; place in slow cooker. Add clam juice; cover and cook on high until fish is tender and flakes with a fork, about 30 minutes. Remove fish, using foil handles; serve with Caramelized Garlic Sauce.

CARAMELIZED GARLIC SAUCE

MAKES 1 CUP (236 ML)

INGREDIENTS

12 cloves garlic
1–2 tablespoons (15-30 mL) olive oil
¾ cup (177 mL) chicken broth, divided
2 tablespoons (30 mL) dry white wine (optional)
1 tablespoon (15 mL) each: all-purpose flour, finely
   chopped parsley
Salt and white pepper, to taste

1. Cook garlic in oil in medium skillet, covered, over medium to medium-low heat until tender, about 10 minutes. Cook, uncovered, over medium-low to low heat until garlic cloves are golden brown, about 10 minutes. Mash cloves slightly with a fork. Add combined broth, wine, and flour; heat to boiling, stirring until thickened, about 1 minute. Stir in parsley; season to taste with salt, and white pepper.

PASTA AND RICE ENTRÉES

ULTIMATE MAC 'N' CHEESE

A combination of four cheeses makes this the best mac 'n' cheese ever! See photo on page 94.

8 SERVINGS

INGREDIENTS

3 cups (708 mL) whole milk
⅓ cup (79 mL) all-purpose flour
1 cup (4 ounces [112 gm]) each: shredded mozzarella and
    Cheddar cheese, crumbled blue cheese
½ cup (2 ounces [56 gm]) Parmesan cheese, divided
1 pound (454 gm) ziti or penne, cooked al dente

1. Mix milk and flour until smooth in large bowl; add remaining ingredients, except ¼ cup (28 gm) Parmesan cheese and ziti. Mix in ziti and spoon into slow cooker; sprinkle with remaining ¼ cup (28 gm) Parmesan cheese. Cover and cook on low 3 hours.

SEVEN-LAYER LASAGNA

It's easy to make lasagna using the "oven-ready" noodles and prepared sauce. This lasagna is delicate in texture, rich in flavor.

6 SERVINGS

INGREDIENTS

3 cups (708 mL) tomato-basil spaghetti sauce
2½ cups (591 mL) ricotta cheese
1 egg, beaten
1 teaspoon (5 mL) dried basil leaves
8 oven-ready lasagna noodles (4 ounces)
2½ cups (10 ounces [285 gm]) shredded mozzarella
    cheese
¼ cup (1 ounce [28 gm]) shredded Parmesan cheese

1. Spread ⅓ cup (79 mL) sauce on bottom of 9 x 5-inch (22.5 x 12.5 cm) bread pan. Combine ricotta, egg, and basil, mixing well. Place 1 lasagna noodle on sauce; top with ⅓ cup (79 mL) each ricotta mixture and mozzarella cheese. Repeat layers, ending with ⅓ cup (79 mL) sauce on top; sprinkle with Parmesan cheese. Place pan on rack in 6-quart slow cooker; cover and cook on low 4 hours. Remove pan and cool on wire rack 10 minutes. The lasagna may look sunken in the center, but will become more even as it cools.

VARIATION

Sausage Lasagna—Make recipe above, adding ¼ cup (59 mL) each sautéed sliced mushrooms (total of 2 cups [473 mL]) and cooked, crumbled Italian sausage between each layer.

WINTER VEGETABLE RISOTTO

Arborio rice is a short-grain rice grown in the Arborio region of Italy. It's especially suited for making risotto, as it cooks to a wonderful creaminess.

4 ENTRÉE SERVINGS

INGREDIENTS

3 cups (708 mL) vegetable broth
1 small onion, chopped
3 cloves garlic, minced
1 cup (236 mL) sliced cremini or white mushrooms
1 teaspoon (5 mL) each: dried rosemary and thyme leaves
1½ cups (354 mL) arborio rice
1 cup (236 mL) each: halved small Brussels sprouts, peeled cubed sweet potato
¼ cup (1 ounce [28 gm]) grated Parmesan cheese
Salt and pepper, to taste

1. Heat broth to boiling in small saucepan; pour into slow cooker. Add remaining ingredients, except Parmesan cheese, salt, and pepper; cover and cook on high until rice is al dente and liquid is almost absorbed, about 1¼ hours (watch carefully so rice does not overcook). Stir in cheese; season to taste with salt and pepper.

VARIATIONS

Summer Vegetable Risotto—Make recipe as above, substituting 4 sliced green onions for the chopped onion, 1 cup (236 mL) chopped plum tomatoes for the mushrooms, and ¾ cup (177 mL) each cubed zucchini and summer yellow squash for the Brussels sprouts and sweet potato.

Italian Sausage and Vegetable Risotto—Make recipe as above, substituting 1 cup (236 mL) each cubed butternut squash and cooked sliced Italian sausage for the Brussels sprouts and sweet potato.

Shrimp Risotto—Make recipe as above, omitting rosemary, Brussels sprouts, and sweet potato; add 1 chopped medium tomato. Stir in ½ cup (118 mL) frozen thawed peas and 8 to 12 ounces peeled, deveined shrimp during the last 15 minutes of cooking time.

ASPARAGUS AND WHITE BEAN PASTA

This can also serve eight as a substantial side dish with grilled or roasted meat. This recipe comes from Sue Spitler, author of 1,001 Best Slow-Cooker Recipes.

4 SERVINGS

INGREDIENTS

1 can (15 ounces [425 gm]) cannellini or Great Northern beans, rinsed, drained

¾ cup (177 mL) vegetable broth

2 cups (473 mL) chopped plum tomatoes

1 cup (236 mL) carrots

1 teaspoon (5 mL) dried rosemary leaves

1 pound (454 gm) asparagus, sliced (2-inch [5-cm] pieces)

Salt and pepper, to taste

8 ounces (224 gm) linguine or thin spaghetti, cooked, warm

¼–½ cup (1–2 ounces [28-56 cm]) shredded Parmesan cheese

1. Combine beans, broth, tomatoes, carrots, and rosemary in slow cooker; cover and cook on high until carrots are tender, about 3 hours, adding asparagus during last 30 minutes. Season to taste with salt and pepper; toss with linguine and cheese.

PAELLA >

Paella, a staple of Spanish cookery, was traditionally prepared with whatever seafood and ingredients the cook had on hand, so the recipe can vary.

4 ENTRÉE SERVINGS

INGREDIENTS

8 ounces (224 gm) chicken tenders, halved
3 ounces (85 gm) Canadian bacon, cut into thin strips
2½ cups (591 mL) reduced-sodium fat-free chicken broth
1 can (14½ ounces [411 gm]) Italian-style diced tomatoes, undrained
1 can (14¾ ounces [418 gm]) artichoke hearts, drained, halved
1 cup (236 mL) each: chopped onion, red and green bell pepper
2 cloves garlic, minced
¾ teaspoon (3.7 mL) each: dried thyme and basil leaves
¼ teaspoon (2.5 mL) crushed saffron threads (optional)
1¼ cups (295 mL) uncooked converted long-grain rice
8 ounces (224 gm) medium shrimp, peeled, deveined
Salt and cayenne pepper, to taste

1. Combine all ingredients, except rice, shrimp, salt, and cayenne pepper, in slow cooker; cover and cook on low 6 to 8 hours, adding rice during last 2 hours, and shrimp during last 10 minutes. Season to taste with salt and cayenne pepper.

SIDE DISHES

REAL MASHED POTATOES

These mashed potatoes are always a knockout, and so easy!

6 SERVINGS

INGREDIENTS

2 pounds (.91 kg) Idaho potatoes, peeled, cooked, warm
⅓ cup (79 mL) each: 2% milk, sour cream
2 tablespoons (30 mL) margarine or butter
Salt and pepper, to taste

1. Mash potatoes or beat until smooth, adding milk, sour cream, and margarine; season to taste with salt and pepper.

SANTA FE BAKED BEANS

These baked beans boast flavors of the great Southwest; modify the amounts of chiles for desired hotness!

8 SERVINGS

INGREDIENTS

1 cup chopped onion
¼–½ cup (59-118 mL) chopped poblano chile or green bell pepper
½–1 serrano chile or jalapeño pepper, finely chopped
2 cans (15 ounces [284 gm] each) pinto beans, rinsed, drained
1 cup (236 mL) whole-kernel corn
6 sun-dried tomatoes (not in oil), softened, sliced
2–3 tablespoons (30-45 mL) honey
½ teaspoon (2.5 mL) each: ground cumin, dried thyme leaves
3 bay leaves
Salt and pepper, to taste
½ cup (2 ounces [56 gm]) crumbled Mexican white or farmer's cheese
¼ cup (59 mL) finely chopped cilantro

1. Combine all ingredients, except salt, pepper, cheese, and cilantro, in slow cooker; season to taste with salt and pepper. Cover and cook on low until beans are desired consistency, 5 to 6 hours, sprinkling with cheese and cilantro during last 30 minutes.

BRAZILIAN BLACK BEAN BAKE

Festive flavors of Brazil combine in this irresistible dish!

12 SERVINGS

INGREDIENTS

2 cups (473 mL) chopped onions
1–2 tablespoons (15-30 mL) each: minced jalapeño pepper, gingerroot
4 cans (15 ounces [284 gm] each) black beans, rinsed, drained
2 cans (14½ ounces [411 gm] each) petite-diced tomatoes, undrained
½ cup (118 mL) each: honey, packed light brown sugar
¾ teaspoon (3.75 mL) each: dried thyme leaves, ground cumin
Salt and pepper, to taste
½ cup (118 mL) each: sliced mango, banana

1. Combine all ingredients, except salt, pepper, mango, and banana, in slow cooker; cover and cook on low until beans are desired consistency, 5 to 6 hours. Season to taste with salt and pepper. Top with mango and banana before serving.

GREEN BEAN CASSEROLE

Reduced-fat ingredients make this old favorite possible in a healthier form.

6 SERVINGS

INGREDIENTS

1 can (10¾ ounces [305 gm]) 98% fat-free cream of mushroom soup
½ cup (118 mL) reduced-fat sour cream
¼ cup (59 mL) 2% reduced-fat milk
1 package (10 ounces [284 gm]) frozen French-style green
  beans, thawed
Salt and pepper, to taste
½ cup (118 mL) canned French-fried onions

1. Mix soup, sour cream, and milk in slow cooker; stir in green
   beans. Cover and cook on low 4 to 6 hours. Season to taste
   with salt and pepper; stir in onions just before serving.

VARIATION >

Green Beans Supreme—Make recipe as above, adding 1 cup (236
mL) sliced sautéed crimini mushrooms and ¼ cup (59 mL) thinly
sliced green onions. Omit French-fried onions; stir in 4 slices
crumbled cooked bacon just before serving.

GREEK-STYLE GREEN BEANS

Fresh green beans are slow cooked with tomatoes, herbs, and garlic in traditional Greek style.

8–10 SERVINGS

INGREDIENTS

1 pound (454 gm) green beans
1 can (28 ounces [794 gm]) petite-diced tomatoes, und-rained
½ cup (118 mL) chopped onion
4 cloves garlic, minced
¾ teaspoon (3.75 mL) each: dried oregano and basil leaves
Salt and pepper, to taste

1. Combine all ingredients, except salt and pepper, in slow cooker; cover and cook on high until beans are tender, about 4 hours. Season to taste with salt and pepper.

WINE-BRAISED CABBAGE

You'll enjoy the combination of aromatic anise and caraway seeds in this cabbage dish.

4–6 SERVINGS

INGREDIENTS

1 medium head cabbage, thinly sliced
¾ cup (177 mL) chopped onion
½ cup (118 mL) chopped green bell pepper
3 cloves garlic, minced
½ teaspoon (2.5 mL) each: crushed caraway and anise seeds
¼ cup (59 mL) each: canned vegetable broth, dry white wine
2 slices diced bacon, cooked crisp, drained
Salt and pepper, to taste

1. Combine all ingredients, except bacon, salt, and pepper, in slow cooker; cover and cook on high until cabbage is tender, 3 to 4 hours. Stir in bacon; season to taste with salt and pepper.

VARIATION

Creamed Cabbage—Make recipe as above, omitting bacon. Stir in combined ½ cup (118 mL) sour cream and 1 tablespoon cornstarch; cover and cook on low 5 to 10 minutes.

GINGER-GARLIC EGGPLANT

Give it a try and see how many times you make it again!

6-8 SERVINGS

INGREDIENTS

3 medium eggplants, unpeeled, cut into cubes (about 12 cups [2.5 kg])

2 medium yellow or red onions, finely chopped

1 (4-inch [10 cm]) piece gingerroot, grated or finely chopped

12 cloves garlic, finely chopped

6–8 green Thai or Serrano chiles, or cayenne peppers, stems removed, chopped

1 heaping tablespoon (20 mL) cumin seeds

1 heaping tablespoon (20 mL) red chili powder

1 tablespoon (15 mL) salt

1 teaspoon (5 mL) ground turmeric

¼ cup (59 mL) vegetable or canola oil

Basmati rice, cooked, warm, for serving

1. Put all ingredients except the oil into the slow cooker. Drizzle the oil over everything and mix thoroughly.

2. Cook on low for 5 hours. If the eggplant begins to look dry while cooking, just drizzle a little more oil into the slow cooker. Serve with the rice.

GINGERED CARROT PURÉE

This traditional French vegetable purée can easily be made in the slow cooker! You'll enjoy its intense flavor and velvety texture.

6–8 SERVINGS

INGREDIENTS

2 pounds (.91 kg) carrots, sliced
2 cups (473 mL) peeled, cubed Idaho potatoes
1 cup (236 mL) water
1–2 tablespoons (15-30 mL) margarine or butter
¼– ½ cup (59-118 mL) 2% milk, warm
½ teaspoon (2.5 mL) ground ginger
Salt and pepper, to taste

1. Combine carrots, potatoes, and water in slow cooker; cover and cook on high until vegetables are very tender, about 3 hours. Drain well. Process carrots and potatoes in food processor until smooth; return to slow cooker. Cook, uncovered, on high until mixture is very thick, about 30 minutes, stirring occasionally. Beat margarine and enough milk into mixture to make a creamy consistency. Stir in ginger; season to taste with salt and pepper.

VARIATIONS

Cauliflower-Fennel Purée—Make recipe as above, substituting cauliflower florets for the carrots, omitting the ground ginger, and adding 1 to 1½ teaspoons (5 to 7.5 mL) crushed fennel or caraway seeds.

Celery Root Purée—Make recipe as above, substituting sliced celery root for the carrots.

Herbed Broccoli Purée—Make recipe as above, substituting broccoli florets for the carrots, and adding ½ teaspoon (2.5 mL) each dried marjoram and savory leaves.

ORANGE-GLAZED BABY CARROTS

The sweet-spiced orange glaze is also delicious over sweet potatoes or beets. This recipe comes from Sue Spitler, author of 1,001 Best Slow-Cooker Recipes.

4 SERVINGS

INGREDIENTS

1 pound baby carrots
¾ cup (177 mL) orange juice
1 tablespoon (15 mL) margarine
½ cup (118 mL) packed light brown sugar
½ teaspoon (2.5 mL) ground cinnamon
¼ teaspoon (1.25 mL) ground mace
2 tablespoons (30 mL) cornstarch
¼ cup (1.25 mL) water
Salt and white pepper, to taste

1. Combine all ingredients, except cornstarch, water, salt, and white pepper, in slow cooker; cover and cook on high until carrots are crisp-tender, about 3 hours. Turn heat to high and cook 10 minutes. Stir in combined cornstarch and water, stirring 2 to 3 minutes; season to taste with salt and pepper.

CORN PUDDING

A great tasting corn pudding, spiked with jalapeño peppers!

6 SERVINGS

INGREDIENTS

1 package (10 ounces [284 gm]) frozen, thawed whole-kernel corn, divided
1 cup (236 mL) whole milk
3 eggs
2 tablespoons (30 mL) all-purpose flour
½ teaspoon (2.5 mL) ground cumin
1 teaspoon (5 mL) salt
¼ teaspoon (1.25 mL) pepper
2 cups (8 ounces [224 gm]) shredded Monterey Jack cheese
¼ cup (59 mL) finely chopped green bell pepper
½–1 small jalapeño pepper, minced

1. Process ¾ cup (177 mL) corn, milk, eggs, flour, cumin, salt, and pepper in food processor or blender until smooth. Pour into greased slow cooker; mix in remaining corn, cheese, bell pepper, and jalapeño pepper. Cover and cook on low until pudding is set, about 3 hours.

CANDIED YAMS

Whether they're called yams or sweet potatoes in your family, the sweet goodness of this dish is the same!

8–10 SERVINGS

INGREDIENTS

2 pounds (.91 kg) sweet potatoes, peeled, sliced (¼-inch [.5 cm])
⅔ cup packed light brown sugar
Salt and pepper
2 tablespoons (30 mL) cold margarine or butter, cut into small pieces
½ cup (118 mL) water
2 tablespoons (30 mL) cornstarch

1. Layer sweet potatoes in slow cooker, sprinkling each layer with brown sugar, salt, and pepper, and dotting with margarine. Combine water and cornstarch and pour over the top. Cover and cook on low 3 hours; increase heat to high and cook until potatoes are tender, about 1 hour.

VARIATION

Fruit and Nut Sweet Potatoes—Make recipe as above, sprinkling ¼ cup (59 mL) each currants or raisins and toasted pecans between layers of potatoes. Sprinkle top of potatoes with ½ cup (118 mL) miniature marshmallows during last 5 to 10 minutes of cooking time.

SWEET POTATO PUDDING >

This comfort food will become a favorite. Drizzle with warm maple syrup, if you like.

6 SERVINGS

INGREDIENTS

Vegetable cooking spray
4 medium sweet potatoes, peeled, cubed
¼ cup (59 mL) orange juice
1–2 tablespoons (15-30 mL) margarine or butter
¼ cup (59 mL) packed light brown sugar
1 tablespoon (15 mL) grated orange zest
¼ teaspoon (1.25 mL) each: ground cinnamon, cloves, salt
3 eggs, lightly beaten
1 cup (59 mL) miniature marshmallows

1. Spray bottom and side of slow cooker with cooking spray and add sweet potatoes; cover and cook on high until potatoes are tender, about 3 hours. Remove potatoes and mash with remaining ingredients, except eggs and marshmallows; mix in eggs. Return potato mixture to slow cooker; cover and cook on high 30 minutes, sprinkling with marshmallows during last 5 minutes.

VARIATION

Sweet Autumn Pudding—Make recipe as above, using 1½ cups (354 mL) each peeled cubed sweet potatoes, hubbard squash, and sliced carrots; substitute ½ teaspoon (2.5 mL) ground mace for the cinnamon and cloves and omit marshmallows.

POTATOES GRATIN

These potatoes taste so rich and creamy, you'll never imagine they were made without heavy cream!

8 SERVINGS

INGREDIENTS

2 pounds (.91 kg) Idaho potatoes, peeled, sliced (¼-inch [.5 cm])
¼ cup (59 mL) thinly sliced onion
Salt and pepper
Cheddar Cheese Sauce (recipe follows)
Ground nutmeg, to taste

1. Layer half the potatoes and onion in slow cooker; sprinkle lightly with salt and pepper. Pour half the cheese sauce over; repeat layers. Cover and cook on high until potatoes are tender, about 3½ hours. Sprinkle with nutmeg.

CHEDDAR CHEESE SAUCE

MAKES ABOUT 2 CUPS (473 ML)

INGREDIENTS

2 tablespoons (30 mL) margarine or butter
3 tablespoons (45 mL) each: finely chopped onion, flour
1½ cups (354 mL) 2% milk
2 ounces (56 gm) processed cheese, cubed
¾ cup (3 ounces [85 gm]) shredded Cheddar cheese
½ teaspoon (2.5 mL) dry mustard
Salt and pepper, to taste

1. Melt margarine in small saucepan; add onion and flour and cook 1 to 2 minutes. Gradually whisk in milk; heat to boiling, stirring until thickened, 2 to 3 minutes. Reduce heat to low; add cheeses and dry mustard, stirring until melted. Season to taste with salt and pepper.

VARIATIONS

Easy Potatoes Gratin—Make recipe as above, omitting Cheddar Cheese Sauce and dividing ¾ cup (3 ounces [85 gm]) shredded Cheddar cheese equally between each layer of potatoes. Pour ½ cup (118 mL) water over and cook as above.

Scalloped Potatoes—Make sauce as above, omitting cheeses and increasing margarine to 3 tablespoons (45 mL), flour to ¼ cup (59 mL), and milk to 2 cups (473 mL).

POLENTA

Creamy polenta is a wonderful side dish—this basic recipe has many possible variations (see below).

6 SERVINGS

INGREDIENTS
¾ cup (177 mL) yellow cornmeal
2 cups (473 mL) water
2 tablespoons (30 mL) margarine or butter
½ cup (2 ounces [56 gm]) grated Parmesan cheese
Salt and pepper, to taste

1. Mix cornmeal and water in slow cooker; cover and cook on high 1½ hours, stirring once after 45 minutes. Stir in margarine and cheese; cover and cook 15 minutes (Polenta should be soft, but should hold its shape). Season to taste with salt and pepper.

VARIATIONS

Blue Cheese Polenta—Make recipe as above, substituting ½ cup (2 ounces [56 gm]) crumbled blue cheese for the Parmesan cheese.

Goat Cheese Polenta—Make recipe as above, substituting ¼ to ½ cup (1 to 2 ounces [28 to 56 gm]) crumbled goat cheese for the Parmesan cheese.

Garlic Polenta—Sauté ¼ cup (59 mL) finely chopped onion and 4 to 6 cloves minced garlic in 1 tablespoon (15 mL) olive oil in small skillet until tender, 2 to 3 minutes. Make recipe as above, omitting Parmesan cheese and adding sautéed vegetables during last 30 minutes of cooking time.

Roasted Pepper–Goat Cheese Polenta—Make recipe as above, omitting Parmesan cheese, and gently stirring ¼ to ½ cup (59 to 118 mL) crumbled goat cheese and ⅓ cup (79 mL) coarsely chopped roasted red pepper into polenta during last 15 minutes of cooking time.

Basil Polenta—Sauté 3 sliced green onions, 2 cloves garlic, and 1 teaspoon (5 mL) dried basil leaves in 2 teaspoons (10 mL) olive oil in large saucepan until tender, about 2 minutes. Make recipe above, adding sautéed mixture during last 30 minutes of cooking time.

INDEX

ABOUT THE SERIES

Each of the books in the *101* series feature delicious, diverse, and accessible recipes—101 of them, to be exact. Scattered throughout each book are beautiful full-color photographs to show you just what the dish should look like. The *101* series books also feature a simple, contemporary design that's as practical as it is elegant, with measures calculated in both traditional and metric quantities.

ABOUT THE EDITOR

Perrin Davis is co-editor of Surrey's *101* series. She lives with her family in suburban Chicago.

Also from Agate Surrey

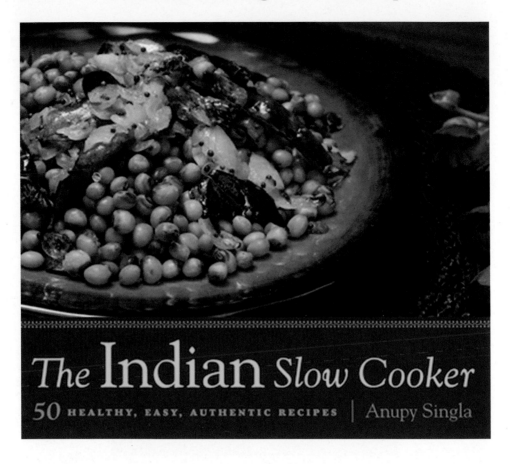

"Singla's book goes against what many believe is required of Indian cuisine—infusing hot oil with a whole mess of spices as the base for dishes. Instead, she argues, throw everything into the Crock-Pot and let the aromatics do their thing ... the book gives old- and new-school cooks alike ample reason to give Indian food a shot."

Janet Rausa Fuller, *Chicago Sun-Times*

ISBN 978-157284-11-16 · $19.95

Available at booksellers everywhere